GOD'S INFINITE WISDOM:

30 DAY DEVOTIONAL

LAKESHA LOWE

GOD'S INFINITE WISDOM: 30 DAY DEVOTIONAL

AUTHOR LAKESHA LOWE

COPYRIGHT © 2025

ALL RIGHTS RESERVED. NO PART OF THIS PUBLICATION MAY BE REPRODUCED, DISTRIBUTED, OR TRANSMITTED IN ANY FORM OR BY ANY MEANS INCLUDING PHOTOCOPYING, RECORDING OR OTHER ELECTRONIC OR MECHANICAL METHODS OR BY ANY INFORMATION STORAGE OR RETRIEVAL SYSTEM WITHOUT THE PRIOR WRITTEN PERMISSION OF THE PUBLISHER EXCEPT IN THE CASE OF VERY BRIEF QUOTATIONS EMBODIED IN CRITICAL REVIEWS AND CERTAIN OTHER NONCOMMERCIAL USES PERMITTED BY COPYRIGHT LAW.

THE BIBLE VERSES USED CAME FROM THE KING JAMES VERSION.

PRINTED IN THE UNITED STATES OF AMERICA
FIRST EDITION.

ALL RIGHTS RESERVED.

ISBN: 9798992558814

DEDICATION

Giving all honor and praise to God for sending Jesus. Thank you.

If you would like to accept Jesus as your personal Lord and Savior, recite the prayer of salvation below:

Jesus, I believe you are the Son of God, that you died on the cross to save me from my sins, death and to restore me to God. I choose now to turn from my sins and every part of my life that does not please you. Thank you Jesus for saving me.

Now that you have accepted Christ as your Savior, find a Christian Church and begin to read your Bible daily.

TABLE OF CONTENTS

DAY 1. WISDOM IS A SPIRIT	pg. 1
DAY 2. REVERENTIAL FEAR	pg. 4
DAY 3. YOUR WISDOM	pg. 7
DAY 4. WISE COUNSEL	pg. 10
DAY 5. TENETS OF WISDOM	pg. 13
DAY 6. WELCOMING WISDOM	pg. 16
DAY 7. SPEECH	pg. 19
DAY 8. PRACTICING RESTRAINT	pg. 22
DAY 9. GUARD YOUR HEART	pg. 25
DAY 10. RIGHTEOUS LIVING	pg. 28
DAY 11. PUTTING GOD FIRST	pg. 31
DAY 12. PATIENCE IS A VIRTUE	pg. 34
DAY 13. EMOTIONS	pg. 37
DAY 14. THE LESS FORTUNATE	pg. 40
DAY 15. DON'T BE LAZY	pg. 43
DAY 16. DISCERNMENT	pg. 46

TABLE OF CONTENTS

DAY 17. APPERANCES	pg. 49
DAY 18. COMMANDMENTS	pg. 52
DAY 19. THE LYING TONGUE	pg. 55
DAY 20. A TRUE FRIEND	pg. 58
DAY 21. MIND CLARITY	pg. 61
DAY 22. NO FEAR	pg. 64
DAY 23. UNDERSTANDING	pg. 67
DAY 24. PATH AND WAYS	pg. 70
DAY 25. SIN	pg. 73
DAY 26. YOU ARE NOT ALONE	pg. 76
DAY 27. FRUITS OF THE SPIRIT	pg. 79
DAY 28. PROMISES OF GOD	pg. 82
DAY 29. COURAGE	pg. 85
DAY 30. GOD IS LOVE	pg. 88

DAY 1: WISDOM IS A SPIRIT

God used wisdom when he created the world (Proverbs 8:22–30). Every facet of creation speaks of God's divine wisdom. With wisdom, the hills, valleys, and depths of the sea were formed. God promises to give you wisdom in your daily life (James 1:5).

DAILY PRAYER

Father, I come before you asking for forgiveness for anything I may have done in thought, word, or action. I repent and acknowledge that you are a just God who forgives when I confess my sins, as written in 1 John 1:9. Lord, I ask that you pour out the spirit of wisdom on me. I want to make wise choices in my daily life.

Your word says in Proverbs 8:35 that those who find wisdom find life and receive your favor. Therefore, I seek your divine wisdom. Help me to make wise

decisions in my words, in how I treat others, and in how I care for myself. In Jesus name, I pray, Amen.

In what areas of your life do you desire more wisdom?

JOURNAL

_____
_____

DAY 2: REVERENTIAL FEAR

Reverential Fear of God Is the beginning of wisdom. Proverbs 9:10 highlights two key indicators of wisdom: reverential fear of God as the beginning of wisdom, and knowledge of God as understanding. This raises the question—are those who do not believe in God considered wise by his standard? The answer is clear: no. Psalm 14:1 and Psalm 53:1 both affirm that those who say "there is no God" are foolish in God's eyes.

If believing in God (and recognizing that Jesus died for us) marks the beginning of wisdom, then unbelievers lack this divine wisdom. While they may possess earthly insight, it does not compare to the wisdom, knowledge, and understanding that God provides. Our belief causes us to rely on our Heavenly Father for everything concerning us, rather than relying solely on ourselves.

Daily Prayer

Lord, thank you for opening my eyes to your Spirit. Jesus, I give you praise and honor! As written in Ephesians 1:17-18, I pray that Jesus Christ gives me the spirit of wisdom and revelation in the knowledge of him, and that I'm enlightened to understand the purpose for which you have called me. Father, help me to focus on your word.

Remove the distractions of this world, and Holy Spirit, silence the suggestions from the kingdom of darkness. As I am enlightened, Father, change my heart and renew my mind so that I may walk in the ways you have called me to. I give you honor and praise. In Jesus name, I pray, Amen.

How do you demonstrate reverence for God?

JOURNAL

DAY 3: YOUR WISDOM

Every day, we make numerous decisions without consulting God. Yet, through his grace and mercy, he continues to watch over us. When making these decisions, are we considering ourselves wiser than God? In fact, we are. With every choice made without seeking him, we are implying that we know best.

As written in Proverbs 3:6-7, we are to acknowledge God in all our ways, and he will direct our paths. The next verse tells us not to be wise in our own eyes. Today, begin incorporating God into your decisions—ask him both the big and small questions, and trust that he will answer.

Daily Prayer

I thank you, Father, for the opportunity to praise and worship you! I magnify your Holy and blessed name, for you are faithful. Lord, I repent for not including you in all my ways. Teach me how to do this. Help me not to lean on my own understanding, so that you can direct my path, as written in Proverbs 3:5-6.

As I go about my day, let your wisdom guide me in making the right choices, keeping my paths straight and protecting me from evil. In Jesus name, I pray, Amen.

Are you seeking God's wisdom before making decisions or choosing paths?

JOURNAL

DAY 4: WISE COUNSEL

Throughout the Bible, we see examples of leaders like Moses and King Nebuchadnezzar seeking wise counsel regarding dreams, visions, or how to approach a specific task. The principle of seeking wise counsel is established right at the beginning of Proverbs, as written in Proverbs 1:5. However, do you know what wise counsel sounds like?

Wise counsel will embody the tenets of wisdom, as described in Proverbs 8:6-8. Wisdom speaks of excellent things, righteousness, truth, and right things. If the counselor is operating in wisdom given by God, then the conversation will reflect all these attributes—nothing wicked or perverse will be discussed.

Daily Prayer

Thank you Heavenly Father for another day. Today I approach your throne to give thanks, honor and request your divine wisdom when listening to people in my life. I ask that you put people after your heart in my life to give me wise counsel on different issues. I also pray that if I am considered wise counsel for someone that the attributes of wisdom saturate the conversation. Change my conversations, make them to edify and uplift those around me. In Jesus name, I pray, Amen.

> Who do you consider to be the wise counsel or counselor in your life?

JOURNAL

_____

_____

DAY 5: TENETS OF WISDOM

When we are first introduced to wisdom (the spirit) in Proverbs, two key principles stand out: knowledge and understanding. Proverbs 8:9-10 highlights the importance of both, emphasizing that knowledge is more valuable than gold. In Proverbs 8:14, it is clearly stated that wisdom is understanding.

These core principles are essential to possessing wisdom, as noted in Proverbs 4:7: "With all thy getting, get understanding." The "and" in this verse indicates that understanding is a requirement. As you apply wisdom in your decisions, ensure that these core tenets— knowledge and understanding—are present in your decision-making process.

Daily Prayer

You are so awesome, God, and I want to take a moment just to reverence you! How great and mighty you are, showing up for me and within me daily. I am thankful for the opportunity to reflect and apply the things I learn through your word to my life. As I navigate this world, I ask that your Spirit rests on me—the spirit of wisdom, understanding, knowledge, and the reverential fear of you. Make me quick to understand, as written in Isaiah 11:2-3. In Jesus name, I pray, Amen.

When seeking Christ throughout your day, how are you applying knowledge and understanding to your decisions?

JOURNAL

DAY 6: WELCOMING WISDOM

Early. This is the time span provided for welcoming God's wisdom into our lives and applying his principles. Proverbs 8:17 highlights how wisdom loves those who seek her early, and those who do will find her. Proverbs 2:2-7 outlines how to welcome God's wisdom into your life.

First, you need to incline your ear, meaning to listen attentively. Then, apply your heart to understanding, meaning to give your undivided attention. The most important step is to ASK God! In Proverbs 2:7, the final point is made clear: It's as simple as asking God because he is the one who gives wisdom.

Daily Prayer

Father, I thank you for today—a day I have never seen before, but you've blessed me to partake in. As I go about my day, please remind me to welcome your wisdom. Fine-tune my ears and make me a great listener to your principles. Soften my heart so I can absorb your word into my spirit. When I hear sound wisdom that pricks my heart, help me to understand and turn from my ways.

Lord, please give me the revelation I need to understand the wisdom you are imparting to me. Without you, I am nothing, and I need you to navigate this journey. Meet me where I am right now. In Jesus name, I pray, Amen.

In what area of your life would you have liked to have had God's divine wisdom?

JOURNAL

DAY 7: SPEECH

Throughout the Proverbs listed in today's devotional, one clear principle stands out: Watch what comes out of your mouth. Proverbs 4:24 tells us to put away perverse or froward language. God is righteous and truth, and neither he nor his wisdom would speak anything contrary to that.

When describing wisdom in Proverbs 8:7-8, it is highlighted that wisdom speaks truth, and the words that proceed from wisdom are righteous. Your speech flows from what is in your heart (mind), as illustrated in Proverbs 16:23: "The heart of the wise teaches his mouth and adds learning to his lips." This profound scripture shows us what the speech of a wise person would be.

Daily Prayer

My Heavenly Father, I love you so much, and I want my conversations to be something you would be pleased to hear. Please forgive me for any perverse words I may have spoken or spoken over someone else. Your word says in 1 John 1:9 that if I confess my sins to you, you are faithful and just to forgive me. I thank you for your forgiveness. Father, please change my heart to be wise so that it may teach my mouth what to say, as it is written in Proverbs 16:23. In Jesus name, I pray, Amen.

Are you able to discern when wisdom is being spoken?

JOURNAL

DAY 8: PRACTICING RESTRAINT

Throughout our days, we interact with people who are going through their own struggles. They may say something that rubs you the wrong way, but sometimes it is best to refrain from responding. Everything does not deserve a response. Proverbs 17:27-28 even tells us to spare our words, and it says that a fool is considered wise when he keeps his mouth shut.

There have been numerous times when I wish I had not said something, but once words are spoken, it is difficult to change the outcome. As you move about your day, practice speaking only truthful and positive statements.

Daily Prayer

Lord, I thank you for the opportunity to praise and magnify your name. You are worthy to be praised. You know my thoughts and the areas of my life that need work. I ask that the Holy Spirit guide me throughout the day, teaching me when to hold my speech. Your word states in Proverbs 17:28 that even a fool is considered wise when he shuts his mouth. Help me to be quiet when needed, and give me discernment about when to speak. In Jesus name, I pray, Amen.

Do you recall any instances in your life where silence should have been exercised?

JOURNAL

DAY 9: GUARD YOUR HEART

Our soul is made up of our mind, will, and emotions. Each day, we are inundated with images and suggestions that shape our thoughts. The Bible tells us in Proverbs 4:23 to protect our heart (mind) with all diligence because, out of it, flow the issues of life. Diligence is used here to show the seriousness with which we should protect our minds.

When our minds are unprotected, many negative seeds can be planted, leading to issues in how we view God and his word for our lives. When your mind is flooded with negative thoughts or images, it can lead to anger, depression, or anxiety, which will affect your day. Jesus further expounds on this in Matthew 12:34b, "For out of the abundance of the heart, the mouth speaks." Today, focus on your thoughts.

Daily Prayer

I thank you Father, for your goodness and many mercies! You are so faithful, and I can trust that your thoughts toward me are good and not evil, and to give me an expected end, as written in Jeremiah 29:11. I ask that you create in me a clean heart (mind) and renew a right spirit within me, as written in Psalm 51:10.

Cleanse me from all unrighteousness and make me over, Father. Outfit me with your armor, starting with the helmet of salvation to protect my mind. Saturate me with the blood of Jesus Christ and keep me as I go about my day. In Jesus' name, I pray, Amen.

What boundaries do you have in place to protect your heart (mind)?

JOURNAL

DAY 10: RIGHTEOUS LIVING

Jesus commanded us to pick up our cross and follow him when we accepted him as Lord over our lives. Each moment of our lives should be intentionally lived, ensuring we honor God and follow his commandments. Did you know that when you live in obedience to God, there are promises? According to Proverbs 10:30, "the righteous shall never be removed;" meaning that wherever God places you, you are established there, and no amount of outside influence can move your placement. When you face trouble in life, the Lord promises that the righteous shall be delivered.

Daily Prayer

Father, I thank you for being my maker, as written in Isaiah 54:12. I worship you because you formed me and placed your breath within me, according to Isaiah 42:5b. You inhabit the praise of your people, and I just want to say thank you, Father! I pray that my life is holy and acceptable to you, and that my daily actions, thoughts, and deeds are viewed as righteous in your sight.

I am so grateful that when I stumble and confess, you are faithful and just to forgive me, purifying me of all unrighteousness, as written in 1 John 1:9. I pray that you keep my mind and spirit rooted in Christ Jesus. In Jesus name, I pray, Amen.

> Does righteous living change with the times, or does it remain the same?

JOURNAL

DAY 11: PUTTING GOD FIRST

Many of us put things and people before God daily. The Lord is clear, from Genesis to Revelation, that he will not share his glory with anyone or anything. In Deuteronomy 5:7-9, the first commandment is that we shall have no other gods before him. Some may think that because they do not have a physical altar, they don't have idols in their lives.

I am here to tell you that this is the deception of Satan. ANYTHING you hold higher than God becomes an idol in your heart. This could be social media, a relationship, or even personal goals. We can easily allow these things to get in the way of our relationship with God. Isaiah 42:8 highlights God's stance on sharing His glory—He will NOT do it. Analyze your actions and words throughout the day to ensure you are keeping God first.

Daily Prayer

I confess that I have placed (insert whatever you have been putting before God) before you, and I am repenting. Cleanse my heart, Lord, renew my mind, as written in Psalm 51:10. I come out of agreement with the idols I have erected in my life and rededicate my heart and spirit back to you. Lord, your word states that your new covenant through Jesus Christ speaks BETTER things about me. Let heaven and earth bear record that I am under the covenant with Jesus Christ. Lastly, Father, change my habits, break cycles, and deliver me from idolatrous ways. In Jesus' name, I pray, Amen.

Can you identify potential idols in your life, and how can you change your behavior to put God first?

JOURNAL

DAY 12: PATIENCE IS A VIRTUE

It can be difficult in life to be patient and wait on the promises of the Lord. Our lack of patience can stem from various things: lack of trust, unbelief, discipline, just to name a few. In our haste, we tend to accept things that God did not originally ordain for us. This, in turn, can lead to hurt, depression, and anxiety because it was not part of God's original plan.

Isaiah 40:31 states, "But they that wait upon the Lord shall renew their strength; they shall mount up with wings as eagles; they shall run, and not be weary; and they shall walk, and not faint." Even in our waiting seasons, we need patience. When you want to give up and do things your way, ask God for patience. It is wise to recognize the need for patience to continue and finish this race called life.

Daily Prayer

Heavenly Father, I come to you today seeking direction in my life. Please forgive me for trying to do things my own way. Your word states in Jeremiah 29:11 that your thoughts toward me are good and that you have an intended plan for my life. Lord, help me to be patient as I walk the paths you have outlined for me. When I feel weary, Lord, renew my strength as stated in Isaiah 40:31. You are such a good Father, and you will exceed whatever I could imagine. In Jesus name, I pray, Amen.

In what areas of your life are you lacking patience?

JOURNAL

DAY 13: EMOTIONS

Each day, we experience a range of emotions, whether they stem from us or others. These emotions can vary from happiness and joy to anger and sadness, depending on what is happening in our environment. We can allow our emotions to derail us or dictate how our day will unfold. A notable example of how an emotion can cause issues is illustrated in Proverbs 10:12, where hatred causes strife among (and within) people.

On the other hand, Proverbs 16:20 shows us that when we handle events wisely and watch our emotions, it will ultimately be for our good. When you trust in the Lord, you are Content! This does not mean that you won't experience negative emotions, but instead, go to God with your feelings and let Jesus carry the burden for you.

Daily Prayer

Lord, please help me to forgive those who have wronged me and not allow my anger to overtake me. Ephesians 4:26-27 tells me it is okay to be angry or upset with a situation, but I must not let that emotion lead me to sin. Father, help me internalize and display the fruits of your Spirit, as listed in Galatians 5:22-23. Guard my heart and spirit. In Jesus name, I pray, Amen.

In your words, what are the differences between the following?

- Jealousy and Envy
- Happiness and Contentment
- Anger and Hatred

JOURNAL

DAY 14: THE LESS FORTUNATE

Did you know that giving to others is a key cornerstone of the ministry of Jesus? God has mandated that we care for the poor, the widow, and the fatherless as early as Deuteronomy 10:18. Throughout the scriptures, we see that through our giving to the poor, we are blessed. Proverbs 19:17 tells us that when we give to the poor, we are giving to God, and he will repay what we give.

It is not our responsibility to control what happens with what is given but to be obedient in giving to those less fortunate than ourselves. When you have the opportunity to give but deliberately turn a blind eye, know that Proverbs 21:13 warns us that in your time of need, you will be ignored as well. Start helping those less fortunate than yourself today.

Daily Prayer

Lord, thank you for all that you have given me. I know that everything I have is because of you. Please forgive me for not looking after those who are less fortunate. I now understand your word, which mandates us to care for the poor.

Bless me, Lord, to be able to give beyond what I have now and give me a heart to help those in need. Help me not to judge others based on what they do not have. Instead, let me give thanks for the opportunity to bless others. In Jesus name, I pray, Amen.

When was the last time you gave (whether money or materials) to someone directly?

JOURNAL

DAY 15: DON'T BE LAZY

How fitting! We are halfway through the devotional, and today's focus is on not being lazy. The Bible refers to laziness as slothfulness or the act of "extended sleep." Of course, God wants us to rest, but there is a limit. When rest interferes with your daily or long-term tasks, it crosses into laziness. Proverbs 20:4 illustrates laziness as a sluggard who refuses to work because of the cold, resulting in no harvest. Proverbs 24:33-34 shows how laziness is like extended sleep which leads to poverty. Get up and work towards your goals. Do not be lazy!

Daily Prayer

Father God, I know that everything is spiritual, and that is how I choose to address the spirit of laziness today. Your word states in Ephesians 1:3 that I am blessed with all spiritual blessings in heavenly places. Lord, give me the desire and focus to pursue all that you have destined for me. Enlighten me, and help me walk according to your calling, as written in Ephesians 1:18. Wake up my earthly helpers to assist me in accomplishing the things you desire of me. Help me, Lord, to develop a lifestyle that encourages productivity. In Jesus' name, I pray, Amen.

What have you been putting off that could be accomplished this week?

JOURNAL

DAY 16: DISCERNMENT

One of the crucial gifts for our daily walk is discernment. Without it, situations can quickly turn from good to bad. There are wise parables that show us how situations may appear one way but are entirely different. In Psalm 55:21, the psalmist describes someone with smooth and flattering words, but in their heart is war.

To recognize this, we need the discernment of the Holy Spirit to reveal their true nature. Proverbs 23:6-7 takes this further by showing how such a person may even feed you, but they have no good intentions for you. Now, more than ever, we need discernment. Ask the Lord to increase your discernment and watch him reveal hidden intentions.

Daily Prayer

Father God, in the name of Jesus, I come to you today just wanting to give you thanks, honor, and praise. There is so much happening in the world today, and I need your discernment in every moment of my life. As I go about my day, I pray that you strengthen me in this area. I pray that the Holy Spirit guides me in my interactions and leads me into all truth, as written in John 16:13. Give me ears to hear and eyes to see what you are saying. In Jesus name, I pray, Amen.

Would you consider your discernment strong in the Lord?

JOURNAL

DAY 17: APPERANCES

In the age of social media and print publications, there is significant emphasis on outward appearances. How we present ourselves to the world is important, but it should never overshadow the work God is doing within us. True beauty shines outwardly when God is changing us from the inside.

Throughout the scriptures, beauty is described as temporary, it does not last forever. 1 Peter 1:24-25 says, "All people are like grass, and all their glory is like the flowers of the field; the grass withers and the flowers fall, but the word of the Lord endures forever." We have all seen flowers and grass wither. Devote time to God's word, for that is the only thing that will last.

Daily Prayer

Father, your word says that you knitted us in our mother's womb, as written in Psalm 139:13, and you know everything about me.

As you renew my mind, I acknowledge that the only thing that will last is your word. Help me navigate a world that is so focused on outward appearances without compromising your truth.

Help me break cycles that misalign with your perfect will for my life. Your word is a lamp to my feet and a light to my path, as written in Psalm 119:105. Continue to guide me, Lord, and sustain my spirit with your living waters. In Jesus' name, I pray, Amen.

> What habits do you practice to ensure you're devoting time to God's word?

JOURNAL

_____

_____

_____

_____

_____

_____

_____

_____

_____

_____

_____

_____

DAY 18: COMMANDMENTS

The commandments of God are something many can readily identify with Christianity. However, we rarely discuss the consequences of operating outside of God's statutes and principles. Some may say that, because of Jesus, we are no longer judged when we stray from God's commandments. But the truth is, operating outside His will leads to death. Matthew 19:17 shows Jesus speaking about the requirements for eternal life, stating we must keep God's commandments. Solomon summarized the whole duty of man in Ecclesiastes: to fear God and keep His commandments.

Daily Prayer

Father God, in the mighty name of Jesus, I thank you for this day. I ask that you lead me throughout my day. Your word states that if I keep your commandments, you will bless me, as written in Deuteronomy 28:1-13. I am confident in your word because, as stated in Psalm 89:34, you will not break your covenant nor alter what you have spoken. Your promises reassure me that as long as I stay focused on you, I will remain on the path you have set for me. Continue to instruct me and teach me in the way I should go, guiding me with your eye, as written in Psalm 32:8. In Jesus name, I pray, Amen.

Do you believe God's commandments are relevant today?

Why or why not, base your answer on scripture.

JOURNAL

DAY 19: THE LYING TONGUE

Most of us were taught not to lie during our formative years. The commandments even state, "Do not bear false witness," in Deuteronomy 5:8. Have you ever noticed that you lie compulsively? If so, it is time to ask the Lord for deliverance from the spirit of lying.

There is no such thing as a "little white lie" or a "big lie"—a lie is a lie, no matter its size. Proverbs 6:16-19 even states that God hates a lying tongue among several other abominations. If you struggle with honesty, ask the Holy Spirit to guide you during conversations and give you the right words during difficult discussions.

Daily Prayer

Lord, I come before your throne seeking forgiveness for the falsehoods I have spoken. My mouth has caused me to stumble in my walk with you, and I ask for your help to change. Set a guard over my mouth and keep watch over the door of my lips, as written in Psalm 141:3. I know nothing is too hard for you, God! Your word states in Psalm 15:4 that a wholesome tongue is a tree of life. Please help me to speak truth with the words of my mouth. In Jesus name, I pray, Amen.

Is there a certain topic you find difficult to be honest about?

JOURNAL

DAY 20: A TRUE FRIEND

The relationships we build with friends can sometimes be stronger than familial bonds, as referenced in Proverbs 18:24. We see this connection clearly in the bond between King David and Jonathan, who loved each other like brothers. There is a saying that "iron sharpens iron," and this is true in our friendships. As you grow in the wisdom of Christ, you will be able to spiritually discern relationships that are ordained by God versus those that are not. Before entering any friendship, be sure that God has given his approval for that relationship.

Daily Prayer

Heavenly Father, I come before your throne of grace asking for your forgiveness and guidance. You are so faithful to me, and I need you every step of the way. As I cultivate friendships, please be at the forefront of every circle I develop. Let those friendships glorify you and edify me in the mighty name of Jesus. Let you get the glory out of all my conversations, and help us uplift one another. I pray I build long-lasting friendships and communities where Jesus Christ is the focus. In Jesus name, I pray, Amen.

When building friendships, how do you incorporate godly wisdom in selecting friends?

JOURNAL

DAY 21: MIND CLARITY

We often take for granted the clarity of mind in our thinking. When we experience situations or relationships that are confusing, it is important to consult God. In him, there is no confusion—he is the author of peace, as written in 1 Corinthians 14:33. Not all decisions will be smooth, but when they come from God, there will be no confusion. He will direct our paths. When we trust in God, he will not confuse us, as stated in Psalm 71:1.

Daily Prayer

Lord, I want to take a moment to say thank you. Thank you for your divine wisdom. I know that you are not the author of confusion, so I ask that you be at the forefront of every situation in my life, leading and guiding me, clearing away confusion, envy, and strife. Let your perfect Shalom rest on me and around me as I go about my day. May the tangible peace of Jesus Christ be felt by those I interact with. I thank you for your grace and mercy, and I ask that your will be done on Earth as it is in heaven, as written in Matthew 6:10. In Jesus name, I pray, Amen.

When you notice envy and strife in situations, do you also notice confusion in those environments? (See James 3:16)

JOURNAL

DAY 22: NO FEAR

First, we must establish that fear is a spirit, and this spirit does not come from God, as stated in 2 Timothy 1:7. Throughout the Bible, we are repeatedly told not to fear. One reason is that fear reveals a lack of trust. God is not only our Creator but the Creator of the universe! We are called to trust him, regardless of our circumstances, because he is greater than any fear.

When we accepted God, he freed us from the bondage of fear and replaced it with his Spirit, as written in Romans 8:15. The phrase "fear not" or "do not be afraid" is one of the most common expressions in the Bible. There is a reason for this—it is God's invitation to trust in his power over our fears.

Daily Prayer

Lord, I repent for allowing fear to drown out your voice, which tells me not to fear. You care for me deeply. You have called the righteous to be as bold as a lion, and I have strong confidence because I fear you. Your word lets me know that I find refuge in you, as written in Proverbs 14:26. I thank you, Jesus, for giving me the power to tread over all evil, and for your promise that nothing shall harm me, as written in Luke 10:19. Today, I renounce the spirit of fear and walk in the fullness of your promises. In Jesus name, I pray, Amen.

In what areas do you allow the spirit of fear to overshadow God's promises? Will you trust God in those areas?

JOURNAL

DAY 23: UNDERSTANDING

We can agree that every good and perfect gift comes from God, including our level of understanding. When we make decisions based on our own limited understanding, we are not walking in the will of God for our lives. Remember that God sees all, and His thoughts towards us are good, as written in Jeremiah 29:11. Sometimes his answers may not be what we expect, but we must trust in his infinite wisdom. He understands the situation far better than we do, and is fully qualified to lead us.

Daily Prayer

Father God, I thank you for this day! As I navigate my choices today, I ask that you grant me the understanding needed to make decisions aligned with your will for my life. Apostle Paul wrote in Ephesians 1:17-18, praying that I would be enlightened with wisdom, revelation, and understanding. I agree with that prayer. Lord, your word in Psalm 2:6 tells me that knowledge and understanding come from your mouth. I trust you to provide divine understanding in every area of my life. In Jesus name, I pray, Amen.

Can you think of a situation where the outcome would have been different if you had consulted God, rather than relying on your own understanding?

JOURNAL

DAY 24: PATH AND WAYS

Throughout the Bible, the phrases "paths" and "ways" are used to describe our habits and choices. In Proverbs 3:6, we are told to acknowledge God in all our ways, and he will direct our paths. When we fail to do so, we often face unpleasant consequences from the paths we choose. However, when we seek God's wisdom in our decision-making, we experience peaceful and pleasant results, as written in Proverbs 3:17. Jesus spoke of the broad and narrow ways, describing how our habits and choices can lead to life or destruction.

Daily Prayer

Heavenly Father, I thank you for waking me up this morning and setting me on the right path. Your word in Psalm 119:105 states that you are a lamp to my feet and a light to my path. I ask that you illuminate my way as I navigate today. Thank you for your divine guidance in my daily decisions. Where I am struggling to change habits, I ask for the Holy Spirit's intervention in Jesus' name. Remind me that I am an overcomer through Christ Jesus and am no longer slaves to my habits. In Jesus name, I pray, Amen.

What are some ways or paths in your life that need to change?

JOURNAL

DAY 25: SIN

As we grow in Christ, the Holy Spirit reveals areas in our lives where unrepented sin, iniquity, or transgressions may still exist. In Psalm 32:5, David writes that when he acknowledged his sin and did not hide his transgressions, the Lord forgave him. True repentance is key to breaking the bondage of sin. It means turning from the actions that led to sin, such as avoiding certain environments or activities.

When we confess our sins, God forgives us and cleanses us of all unrighteousness, as written in 1 John 1:9. Though we are not perfect and will make mistakes, we can always ask for forgiveness from God and forgive ourselves. Remember, there is no condemnation for those in Christ Jesus, as written in Romans 8:1.

Daily Prayer

Lord, I thank you for this new day and for deliverance from the shackles of sin. Your word says that if I confess my sins, you are just and faithful to forgive me and cleanse me of all unrighteousness. For that, I am truly thankful. Where I struggle with sin, I ask for your divine intervention. I cannot do this alone; I need the blood of Jesus Christ to cleanse me and transform my heart. I desire a heart after you, God, in the name of Jesus. Let the fruits of your Spirit be evident in my daily life. In Jesus name, I pray, Amen.

Is there an area in your life where you struggle with sin? If so, have you repented, and are you changing the habits that lead you into sin?

JOURNAL

DAY 26: YOU ARE NOT ALONE

It is easy to feel alone at times, but one of the greatest comforts we have in God is the assurance that we are never alone. As a believer in Christ Jesus, do you realize the immense spiritual support surrounding you? Psalm 34:7 tells us that the angel of the Lord encamps around those who fear Him, and their job is to deliver us. Psalm 91:11-12 highlights how angels are assigned to protect us from harm. The most beautiful thing about Jesus' ascension to heaven was that He left us with a Comforter. He knew we would need Him, and He ensured we would never be alone.

Daily Prayer

Heavenly Father, I ask that you watch over me today as I go about my daily activities. Help me to always remember that I am never alone in this journey called life. I thank You,

Holy Spirit, for being present and dwelling inside of me. I thank You, Jesus, for being my High Priest and interceding on my behalf. When I feel alone, I ask that your ministering spirits (angels) speak to my heart and encourages me, for I am an heir of salvation, as written in Hebrews 1:14. In Jesus name, I pray, Amen.

Do you pray for the comfort of the Holy Spirit when you feel lonely?

JOURNAL

DAY 27: FRUITS OF SPIRIT

Fruits are mentioned throughout both the Old and New Testaments. In Matthew 7:15-20, Jesus uses fruit metaphorically to reveal a person's true character, saying that a tree is known by its fruit. The mask of falsehood can only last so long before it slips. Every Christian who follows Christ should exhibit the Fruit of the Spirit. We should desire to show love, joy, peace, forbearance, kindness, goodness, faithfulness, gentleness, and self-control. These qualities are the very attributes that draw us closer to God.

Daily Prayer

Father God, in the name of Jesus, I thank you for this new day that you have made. I thank you for your Holy Spirit, and I strive to embody the Fruit of Your Spirit. Lord, I ask for a fresh outpouring of your anointing, that when people meet me today, your light shines through me. I pray that the Fruit of the

Spirit is deeply rooted in my soul. Holy Spirit, thank you for teaching, guiding, and molding me into dedicated disciple of Christ. In Jesus name, I pray, Amen.

In your walk of faith, do you display any of the characteristics mentioned? If so, which ones?

JOURNAL

DAY 28: PROMISES OF GOD

Throughout the Bible, God makes many promises to his servants. At times, we may lose sight of these promises when we focus on our immediate circumstances. John 3:16 is a promise that has transformed generations. It reveals the magnitude of God's love—that he gave his only Son to save us. By believing in Christ Jesus, we are promised eternal life. Psalm 91 is a beautiful representation of God's promise to be our protector and our refuge in times of trouble. Let us reflect on his promises throughout our day today.

Daily Prayer

Lord, I just want to thank you! As I go about my day, help me to be ever mindful of the promise you made when your Son died for me on Calvary. Thank you, Jesus, for the ultimate sacrifice you made for my sins. Father God, I honor ou, and I give you all the glory. In Jesus name, I pray, Amen.

Do you have a promise of God that you meditate on?

JOURNAL

DAY 29: COURAGE

The Bible highlights the struggles the children of Israel faced due to their failure to keep their covenant with God. Israel also struggled with courage in the face of opposition. The Lord would consistently remind them of who he is and who they are to him. We are not much different today! Psalm 27:14 states that if we wait on the Lord and are of good courage, he will strengthen our hearts. Despite any physical circumstances, remember that you are an heir of God, which comes with all the privileges. Remind yourself of Isaiah 40:29, which tells us that God gives power when we are faint.

Daily Prayer

Lord, I thank you today for giving me courage and for supporting me in difficult situations. Father, you know the areas where I need courage, and I ask that you strengthen me. Give me the words to say and the wisdom to know when to say them.

Lord, I also pray that you give me the confidence to do the hard things and have the tough conversations. Thank you for being present with me in every moment. I give you praise, glory, and honor. In Jesus name, I pray, Amen.

Where have you needed courage lately? Family, work, etc.?

JOURNAL

DAY 30: GOD IS LOVE

As we wrap up this 30-day devotional, I want to remind you today that God loves us. No matter where you are in life, he truly cares for you. In Ephesians 2:4-7, we see how he extended his mercy toward us when we were still in sin. God awakened us from the world and the devices of the enemy, and now, by grace through Christ Jesus, we are seated in heavenly places. Let us move intentionally each day in love because God is love, as written in 1 John 4:8.

Daily Prayer

Heavenly Father, as this 30-day devotional ends, I pray that your unmatched love permeates every moment of my day. I pray that you continue to surround me with your love. Lord, as I go into the world, may others experience your love at every turn. Father, I pray that you pour your love upon me and that your tangible peace, your Shalom, rests on me in the mighty name of Jesus. I praise you for your mercy and grace, which gives me

the opportunity today to get it right again. In Jesus name, I pray, Amen.

Can you remember the first time you experienced God's love?

JOURNAL

www.ingramcontent.com/pod-product-compliance
Lightning Source LLC
Chambersburg PA
CBHW070206100426
42743CB00013B/3075